The Jenkins Family (Lifestyle and Routines)

Ra Vega Torres

Bluebell Publishing

Title Page

The Jenkins Family – (Lifestyle and Routines)– Ra Vega Torres

Published September 2020

Copyright © 2020 by Nick Monks (Ra Vega Torres)

All rights reserved. No part of this publication may be reproduced, distributed, or transmitted in any form or by any means, including photocopying, recording, or other electronic or mechanical methods, without the prior written permission of the publisher, except in the case of brief quotations embodied in critical reviews and certain other non- commercial uses permitted by copyright law.

Printed by Lulu
www.lulu.com

ISBN: 978-1-8381263-6-0

For Amanda, Karl, Saskia

Credits-Front Cover Image- Dominika Rose Clay- Pexels-977739

CONTENTS

Afternoon Leisure   Page 9
Waking Up Time   10
Susan, The Jenkins Bedtime   11
The Lounge, Evening   12
The Sons "A" Levels   13
Susan, Dave   14
Lake District 1   15
Jess Visit- Mark   16
The Wedding Event   17
Corona Virus   18
The Mundane   19
Gardening   20
Going Out   21
Thinking Time   22
Dog Walking 1   23
The Lake District   24
Work Contracts Dave   25
Sitting in the Garden or Conservatory   26
Night- Time   27
Janice Visits   28
Susan Alone, Holiday   29
Dog Walking 2   30

The Jenkins – (Lifestyle and Routines)

Afternoon Leisure

Its 2pm. Susan sits in the lounge
She likes this period of quiet
When Dave is at work. And Tom
At college. The house perfunctorily
Tidied. Sitting in the lounge with the curtains
Partially open. Slipping into the kitchen
To eat snacks. Tom arrives back at 5pm
Dave at 6pm. The dog greets them first
Then Susan tells them what Janice and Marg said
When she visited them.

Waking Up Time

The alarm clock chimes in the bedroom
Then five minutes later in Toms room

Susan is the first to wake
Dave then quickly follows her

They pour scorn on Nick next door who sleeps during the day
And is awake during the night

Tom reluctantly rises
And in the kitchen they have toast and butter

The dog is awaiting them
Tom drives to college in the Red Astra
His parents bought him

The bathroom rota is Dave first
Tom second
Susan when the other two have left the house

Dave goes to work. Tom goes to college
Susan takes the dog for a walk.

Susan, The Jenkins Bedtime

Today at 9pm. She undresses. Puts on her pyjamas
And sits in the lounge for a coffee
Her husband and son are already in bed
She enters the bedroom and gets beneath the quilt
She doesn't like physical contact between her and her husband Dave
So keeps away from him on the far side of the double bed
Sleeping patterns involve ignoring each other
As if the other doesn't exist
She sleeps on her side. And drags the quilt over her
By rote her husband lets her have most of the duvet and bed.

The Lounge- Evening

Dave sits on the edge of the sofa
And Susan semi lies taking two seats
Her son sits on the armchair
He is not allowed to dangle a leg over the arm- chair sides
Neither talk to each other
The television is switched to Susan's channel
A programme tele shopping about clothes
Bizarre as Susan only dresses demurely
In jumpers and baggy jeans
Each is starring into space. While the silence hums
In unison with the fridge freezer growl.

The Son's "A" Levels

The son's Tom's A levels are in three months
Its 7pm
"Go and study" says Susan
"Nor" says tom. *"Go and study." "Nor"*
He grumpily goes into his bedroom
And sits at the desk his parents bought him
He opens the folder with notes
Chews on gum
And looks at his mobile phone
To see if Jake has texted him
His mother appears at the doorway
Throws a cushion at him
And shouts. *"Study Tom" "Not the phone"*
Falling short of taking the phone off him
She composes herself. Then goes to the kitchen
And makes a cup of coffee with warm milk.

Susan, Dave

Its 2pm. Dave's off to the groceries.
And to take Ralph the dog for a walk
In Brickcroft nature reserve

Their son Thomas is still at college
Susan sits in the lounge on the phone to Shell
The phone call could last 30 minutes

When Dave comes back
Tom is also back
And Dave manoeuvres the cars
So all three will sit on the drive

Then they have tea. Salmon and salad
And potato salad
Connect the HMDI cable to the TV

And go on friends facebook pages
Look at hotels in Scottish highlands
Tele shop for fridge freezers.
And look at the symptoms of corona virus.

Lake District 1

They open the back door for Ralph
And drive away to the southern lakes
They don't bag fells
They find a wood and hill near the south of lake Windermere
And putting on coats (it is March)
Walk along the path into the wood
Ralph careers sprinting in front
And they notice buds and late berries on trees
A squall of temporary rain
Alder just coming into leaf
A stream cascading by the side of the path
Chaffinch alighting on the gravel path
A blackbird with yellow eyes darts across
Ralph comes back to master and mistress
And the tussock grass
Gives under their boots as they climb the low hill.

Jess Visit - Mark

Jess arrives. They have known each other-
For 22 years
And sit chatting about relatives
And common acquaintances
Jess offers Susan advice on Mark
Who's *"just impossible"*
Jess says he should look after himself better
He recently split from his wife Davina
And further nobody's seen Davina for two months
The assumption is Davina has gone to her parents in London
"But why doesn't she ring" says Susan
Anyway Mark needs to be a man and self care
"And to be less rude and obnoxious"

Outside sun plays on the garden shrubs
And Dave is watering them with the hose pipe
Jess and Susan eat a natural Greek yogurt each and laugh.

The Wedding Event

Chrissies wedding is looked forward to
The three of them wake in the morning
And potter about the house- It is a Saturday

Susan says. *"Lets dress"* Tom and Dave put on suits
And Susan puts on the green dress
From the box she bought three weeks ago from Dorothy
Perkins

At the reception they sip fruit juice and then wine
Chatting to many of the people they have known for years
The event is on the lawn of a church

Tables have snacks and tit bits to eat
The cheery introductions are good.
More contentious conversation topics are
Tactfully ignored

The newly married couple circulate
And Susan and Dave chat to other guests
There son Tom joins with two former playing friends
Susan and Dave stand at the side as speeches are made

At home they collect the dog Harry from the aunt
And still in finery open the windows and watch the clouds
Scud across a spacious sky.

Corona Virus

Society has closed down
Dave and Susan potter in their garden
Behind the walled gate
Put in place so Harry the dog couldn't stray
Spring is unfurling in tree buds
And the street is indoors
Dave washes the cars for this week
Inside again. The dishwasher is loaded
And switched on
The dog Harry runs into the lounge.

The Mundane

A line of shoes on the kitchen doorstep
Drear silence of the house
Grumpily doing housework
A burp at the potatoes and mayonnaise
Time for gossip with Janet
Washing the car again, then again
Blaming the guy next door
An argument between mother and son
Then going to the grocers for £80 of food.

Gardening

Susan sits in the lounge watching tv
Dave goes out to wash the three cars
He applies the water from a hose pipe
Measuredly adds cleaning fluid
Cleaning cars takes two hours
He does this once a week

The next day he takes the water pipe out
And waters the shrubs in the front garden

Susan never ventures out to do the gardening
And her husband and son. Are her swords.

Going Out

They go out eight times a day
To the groceries
Three times a day to take their dog for a walk
Visiting and being visited by relatives and friends
The rest of the time they spend pottering-
About in their garden- front and back.

Thinking Time

Susan uses her time in doors often
To think about neighbours
Striving people who pursue their own benefit
Susan is unconcerned about others welfare.

Dog Walking 1

They take their dog for a walk for
The second time that day
As there walking around Brickcroft nature reserve
Other people with dogs
Stop and chat to them
Susan often takes Dave or Tom
For protection. They know every nature reserve
And countryside area in the Penwortham
And western parishes area. And further afield.

The Lake District 2

They go to the Lakes. It's a Saturday
To take their dog for a walk
They go to the Lakes or Yorkshire Dales often
They don't bag fells
They find a countryside place
Today a wood and hill
Near to Ambleside
Walk their dog for one hour
They don't have a pub lunch or take photos
They drive straight back to Longton, Preston.

Work Contracts, Dave

Dave is now working from home
Doing contracts for Britten Norman
An aircraft manufacturer in Chester
Also based in other places around the world
He leases and sells Islander light aircraft
To customers and arranges the customer
Specifications of the aircraft.

Sitting in the Garden or Conservatory

A warm early May day
The housework is done. And Susan, Dave, and Tom
Sit at a table on three white plastic chairs
In the garden. The lawn is mowed short
Flowers bloom in the early summer
And tits and finches flit from one garden to the next
They chat lightly. Sip three cups of decaffeinated ground coffee
Reel at the noise of drilling coming from somewhere
The noise abates
And they sequester in the breeze
Blown in across the Fylde plain from the Irish sea.

Night-Time

Susan is in bed, next to Dave
She moves onto her side
Dave stirs slightly
Both stay asleep
In the back- bedroom Tom is sleeping
He snores lightly
The dog sleeps in the basket
In the lounge curled up
Dark sheets and invades the corners of the house
Each- others dreams encircle each other
And they await the habitual alarm clock at 6.30 am.

Janice Visits

Janice comes round with a new handbag
She bought from a boutique in blackpool
She also bought a make-up pouch
Containing lipstick / eye mascara/ blusher
Susan has known Janice for 24 years
They laugh together
And reminisce about the joint family holiday to Cornwall

Susan tells Janice of Dave, Tom sand Shaun's visit to Berlin
Janice likewise has known Susan for 24 years
They make ground coffee
And chat about tom Susan's son
And Elizabeth, Janice's daughter
On TV they watch various channels
Before watching tele shopping
Then turn off the tv
And go to a café and have cake and cappuccino
They go back to Susan's and chat some more
Before goodbyes and the promise to keep in touch.

Susan Alone, Holiday

Dave is in Berlin. With her son and his friend Shaun
Susan watches tv
Takes the dog for a walk
And sits in the conservatory with a fruit juice
She thinks of the new kitchen and how
Smart it looks
And goes to the supermarket to buy groceries.

Dog Walking 2

Traipsing the same road, the same path
To Brickcroft nature reserve in Longton, Preston
The dog Ralph gets three walks a day
The lakes are walked around
There are two of them
And they look sat the swans, mallards, and coots
Dogs have to be kept on a lead at all times
The dog Ralph is a whippet
Dave/Susan/Tom take him for a walk
Usually singularly, occasionally together
Sometimes they drive to the lakes
Or other countryside areas to take Ralph for a walk
In communion with the other dog walkers
Comparing pet dogs
Watching the mallards by the bank of the two lakes.

www.ingramcontent.com/pod-product-compliance
Lightning Source LLC
Chambersburg PA
CBHW051720040426
42446CB00008B/982